101 Amazing Things to Do in California

© 2018 101 Amazing Things

All rights reserved. No part of this publication may be reproduced, distributed, or transmitted in any form or by any means, including photocopying, recording, or other electronic or mechanical methods, without the prior written permission of the publisher, except in the case of brief quotations embodied in critical reviews and certain other noncommercial uses permitted by copyright law.

Introduction

So you're going to California huh? You are very lucky indeed! You are sure in for a treat because California is one of the most magical places in the United States, and indeed the world, for young and old, backpackers and luxury travellers alike.

This guide will take you on a journey from the major cities like Los Angeles and San Francisco, through to hidden beaches and national parks.

In this guide, we'll be giving you the lowdown on:
- the very best things to shove in your pie hole, from the best of LA's food truck scene through to a 19th century soda fountain
- incredible festivals, whether you would like to party hard in the desert or you'd prefer to chow down at an annual strawberry festival
- the coolest historical and cultural sights that you simply cannot afford to miss from world-class museums to Scandinavian style mansions

- the most incredible outdoor adventures, whether you want to try out surfing in Malibu, or you want to climb to dramatic mountain peaks in Yosemite National Park.
- the places where you can party like a local and make new friends
- and tonnes more coolness besides!

Let's not waste any more time – here are the 101 most amazing, spectacular, and coolest things not to miss in California!

1. Spot Your Idols on the Hollywood Walk of Fame

California might just be home to more celebrities and iconic figures than anywhere else in the world, and you can see all the most impressive Hollywood stars for yourself on the Hollywood walk of fame. The walk of fame runs for over 2 kilometres, and around 2500 stars have been added to the pavement since its inauguration in 1958. Stars you'll be able to spot include James Dean, Elton John, and Bob Marley, among many others. *(Hollywood Blvd; www.walkoffame.com)*

2. Visit the Very Unique Glass Beach

We all know that pollution is a bad thing, but there is one particular spot in California where historic pollution has actually created a rather beautiful man-made formation. In the earlier part of the 20th century, the Fort Bragg coastal area was sadly used as a dumping site. During this time tonnes of glass were deposited into the ocean, but over the years since then, the glass has been broken down and eroded to become like small glass pebbles, which completely fill up the beach, and although it's man-made (with some help from the ocean) it looks really quite magical.

3. Say Hi to the Animals at San Diego Zoo

If you are an animal lover, visiting zoos while on a trip away can be a point of contention because not all zoos have the same ethical standards. Fortunately, you don't have to have anything to worry about at San Diego Zoo, which pioneered open air, cageless exhibits that replicate natural habitats, and it's one of few places that successfully breeds endangered giant pandas. In the zoo, you'll find more than 650 animal species in zones such as the monkey trails, the panda trek, and the tiger river.
(2920 Zoo Dr, San Diego; http://zoo.sandiegozoo.org)

4. See the Stars at the Samuel Oschin Planetarium

The Samuel Oschin Planetarium, located in the Griffith Observatory in Los Angeles, is often considered to be the greatest planetarium in the whole world. With its star projector, digital projection system, state of the art aluminium dome, and surround system this hardly seems

surprising. Make sure you check out their Centred in the Universe show, which takes visitors on a magical journey of cosmic exploration.
(2800 E Observatory Rd, Los Angeles; http://griffithobservatory.org/programs/soplanetarium.html)

5. Eat Breakfast in Ice Cream Form at Humphry Slocombe Ice Cream

One of the loveliest things about visiting California is the climate, but with that year round sunshine, you might need something to cool you down now and again, and what better way to cool down than with a towering mound of ice cream? Well, for an ice cream that you won't forget in a hurry, we recommend heading down to Slocombe Ice Cream in San Francisco where they serve a secret breakfast flavour with bourbon and cornflakes. Yum!
(2790 Harrison St, San Francisco; www.humphryslocombe.com)

6. Explore Griffith Park on Horseback

California is a nature lover's paradise, and there's even swathes of green land in the major cities like Los Angeles, where you can find the epic Griffith Park, a green space

that covers a mighty 4310 acres of land. There are many ways to get back to nature in the park, but we think that exploring the land via horseback is one of the ways to have a truly memorable experience. There are a number of guided trails that are priced at around $25 per hour.
(4730 Crystal Springs Dr, Los Angeles; www.laparks.org/griffithpark)

7. Go Night Paddle Boarding on Newport Beach

The bay of Newport Beach is a very popular place for paddle boarding, but what makes the paddle boarding stand out from any regular experience is that tour companies here often take people out on to the water at night. You will explore the water with a special paddle board with LED lights so that the water becomes beautifully illuminated. This means you will be able to find your way as you paddle, and that you can see some of the stunning marine life below the water too.

8. Try a Sushi Burrito at the Jogasaki Truck

California is a cosmopolitan place, so when you're in the state you won't just be restricted to eating classic

American grub. There are tonnes of food trucks that serve up ethnic cuisine, and we particularly like the trucks that serve up foods of contrasting styles and flavours. The Jogasaki Truck in Santa Monica is one not to miss with its interesting mix of Japanese and Mexican cuisine. The sushi burrito is particularly yummy, with burrito ingredients wrapped up into sushi rice.

(www.jogasakiburrito.com)

9. Take a Ride on the Napa Valley Wine Train

If you have a taste for wine, your trip to California will be extremely rewarding, and particularly if you spend plenty of time in Napa Valley, which is the Californian wine country. Without a doubt, the most luxurious way of exploring this region is by taking a ride on the Napa Valley Wine Train. On this journey, you get to ride in an antique train, eat gourmet food, watch the incredible Napa Valley scenery roll past, and of course, sip on the very best wines that the region has to offer.

(1275 McKinstry St, Napa; http://winetrain.com)

10 Go Camping in Yosemite National Park

If you had the idea that California is a place defined by the glitz and glamour of Hollywood, you can think again, because actually the west coast state has far more to it than just that. Something that should be on the bucket list of every nature lover who makes their way to California is Yosemite National Park, a park that covers a staggering expanse of 750,000 acres. In our opinion, the best way to immerse yourself in the plains, mountains, and rivers is to go camping there, which is possible all year round but particularly popular from July to September.
(www.nps.gov/yose/index.htm)

11. Watch the LA Philharmonic at the Walt Disney Concert Hall

Because of its name, you might expect the Walt Disney Concert Hall to host cheesy shows for kids, but this is far from the case. In fact, this is one of the most acoustically impressive concert halls in the whole world, it's home to the LA Philharmonic Orchestra, and it's a place where you can take in incredible classical and jazz shows. The LA Philharmonic are considered to be one of the most forward thinking and innovative orchestras in the world, so be sure to keep up to date with their schedule.

(111 S Grand Ave, Los Angeles; www.laphil.com)

12. Wave a Rainbow Flag for San Francisco Pride

It goes without saying that San Francisco is one of the most gay friendly places on the face of the planet, not just in the United States, and that any LGBT traveller will have an incredible time in this trendy Californian city. While this is a super gay-friendly place at any time of the year, it really comes alive during the San Francisco Pride Festivities, which take place at the end of June each year. The highlight is a huge street parade that is filled with colour, music, and dancing.

(www.sfpride.org)

13. Learn How to Surf in Malibu

California has a reputation as one of the top surfing destinations anywhere in the world, and that's with good reason. But as a new visitor to the state, it can be hard to know where to go to ride the best waves. Truthfully, there are lots of places along the coast that have great surf, but we recommend checking out the waves in Malibu. Just 12 miles west of Los Angeles, Malibu has a number of surf schools that can cater to total beginners, and where you can rent everything you would need to ride the waves.

14. Go Dinosaur Crazy at the Natural History Museum of Los Angeles County

Travelling with kids can be tough because they need to be kept entertained at all times. Well, the Natural History Museum of Los Angeles County is somewhere they will be entertained and learn new things at the same time. Covering 4.5 billion years of history with 35 million artefacts, this place is impressive to say the least, and it's always the Dinosaur Hall that steals the show. Inside, you'll find a series of life size T-Rex.
(900 Exposition Blvd, Los Angeles; www.nhm.org)

15. Discover Ancient Fossils at La Brea Tar Pits

Los Angeles is a city that might surprise you, because it's not all Hollywood and neon lights. Actually, this is a great place for history buffs and nature lovers as well. For one of the most unique places in California, and indeed the world, you need to head to the La Brea Tar Pits, which are pits that have formed over tens of thousands of years from asphalt seeping up out of the ground. Animal fossils are often preserved in the tar, and some of these can be seen in the site's associated museum.

(5801 Wilshire Blvd, Los Angeles; www.tarpits.org)

16. Fill Your Stomach at Eat Drink SF

San Francisco is, without a doubt, a gastronomic city. But if your budget doesn't stretch to eating out in the best of the city's restaurants every day, you can get a comprehensive taste of what San Francisco has to offer at the Eat Drink SF event, which is hosted each year at the end of August. At this event, you can try the signature dishes of more than 35 local restaurants, and sip on beers, wines, and spirits from local producers and merchants. You can also attend cooking classes, and watch celebrity chefs speak.

(http://eatdrink-sf.com)

17. Party Hard at Coachella

If summer festivals are one of your favourite things, you will have heard lots about Coachella already. This annual music and arts festival takes over the Coachella Valley in

April every year, and has a bohemian and very welcoming atmosphere. As well as performances from major music acts, you can expect art viewings, art workshops, circus and theatre performances, delicious food, shopping markets, and more.

(www.coachella.com)

18. Take in a Stellar View of Los Angeles from LA City Hall

Los Angeles is a sprawling city with many different districts, and it's very hard to get a sense of the sprawling nature of the city when you are walking along the streets. Instead, you need a bird's eye view, and the best place for this is from the observatory at LA City Hall. The city hall is very much operational and houses the mayor's office too. The observatory is open to the public during the working hours between Monday and Friday, and it's totally free to check it out.

(200 N Spring St, Los Angeles)

19. Relax With a Movie at Grauman's Egyptian Theatre

There is tonnes to do around California, but there will be times when all you want to do is watch a great movie. When that moment strikes, you need to know about Grauman's Egyptian Theatre. This lavish cinema is no ordinary place to watch a film because it has served an important role in Hollywood for almost a century. It was actually at this cinema that the first ever Hollywood film premiere took place.

(6712 Hollywood Blvd, Los Angeles; http://egyptiantheatre.com/egyptian/egypt.htm)

20. Walk Across the Golden Gate Bridge

When you picture San Francisco in your head, what is it that you see? If an image of the Golden Gate Bridge pops up, this would be no surprise, because this is one of the most iconic bridges in the whole world. Of course, taking a selfie with the bridge in the background is practically obligatory. But did you know that you can also walk the 3 mile length of the bridge? It's a great way to see the city and get some exercise at the same time.

(www.sftravel.com/golden-gate-bridge)

21. Be Wowed by the Highest Waterfall in North America, Yosemite Falls

There's a huge number of things to see inside Yosemite National Park, but the most popular of all the places might just be Yosemite Falls, and this is not least because it happens to be the highest waterfall in all of North America, with a height of 2450 feet. The waterfall is so big that there are three tiers to the falls, and for the very best view, do make the effort to take the trail to the upper falls. Nature lovers won't regret it.

(www.nps.gov/yose/planyourvisit/waterfalls.htm)

22. Take a Scenic Drive Along Death Valley's Badwater Road

California is very much roadtrip country, and a drive through Badwater Road, otherwise known as Death Valley, will certainly be a drive to remember. This drive contains some of the highest temperatures and lowest elevations in the world, which make the landscapes incredibly unique, and ideal for exploring within the confines of an air conditioned vehicle. On the drive you'll spot steam explosions that have caused carved craters, saltwater flats, and more.

23. Get Away From It All at Pfeiffer Beach

There is so much stunning coastline around California that it can be hard to know where to start your beach adventure. There are plenty of spots for surfing and playing volleyball, but what if you simply want to get away from it all and enjoy the natural beauty of your surroundings? In that case, we recommend Pfeiffer Beach. This beach is very hard to find, but that's what makes it special. Once you get there, you'll be greeted by a wide sandy beach and calm waters for swimming undisturbed by watersports enthusiasts.

24. Sip on Cocktails on The Upstairs at Ace Hotel

There's certainly no shortage of places in Los Angeles for anyone to grab a cocktail, but if you want to have a decadent cocktail and a stellar view of the whole city, you need to make your way to the rooftop of the famous Ace Hotel. There is also a rooftop pool, and all you need to access it is to buy a drink. Unlike other rooftop bars that are only open to guests, you can chill out here without breaking the bank.

(929 S Broadway, Los Angeles; www.acehotel.com/losangeles/upstairs)

25. Challenge Yourself by Hiking Mount Whitney

Mount Whitney is the highest mountain on the mainland of the United States, and that means two things. First of all, it's beautiful to look at. And secondly, it's an epic climb that even adventurous travellers might be wary of. But if you are a daredevil through and through, the good news is that climbing this beautiful mountain is certainly not impossible. The trek is 11 miles so it can actually be done in a day, just be sure to wear some warm clothes because it gets chilly at the top of a 14,500 foot mountain.

26. Connect With Nature at the Conservatory of Flowers

Yes, San Francisco is a happening place with tonnes of cool eateries and bars, but if you are in need of a little peace and tranquillity on your visit, a leisurely morning spent in the Conservatory of Flowers would be a very smart idea. This greenhouse and botanical garden is a relic of the city that dates back to 1879, and inside you can find a stunning collection of high altitude orchids, beautiful water lilies, tropical crops such as banana and vanilla, and loads more besides.

(100 John F Kennedy Dr, San Francisco; www.conservatoryofflowers.org)

27. Catch a Live Show at the Hollywood Fringe Festival

Hollywood is, of course, well known as the entertainment capital of the world. But beyond the mega-celebrities and pop star icons, there's a creative scene in Hollywood that is far more edgy, and you can check it out at the Hollywood Fringe Festival, which is hosted in June each year across many of the coolest venues in this part of Los Angeles. There are hundreds of shows being staged at this time, so it's a great opportunity to see some up and coming theatre, whether you're into contemporary dance, musicals, or straight plays.

(www.hollywoodfringe.org)

28. Have an Off-Road Adventure on the Algodones Sand Dunes

There is so much diverse terrain within California that in the south part of the state you can even find sand dunes. The Algodones dunes are located close to the Arizona border and extend for 45 miles. The dunes here are very hilly and soft, and that makes them difficult to explore on foot (particularly when there is no shade), but one of the more popular ways of exploring this beautiful landscape is in a 4x4 or dune buggy. There are local tour companies that can take care of the whole experience for you.

29. Walk the Rugged Coastline of Mendocino Headlands State Park

There is a tonne of beauty to be discovered on the Californian coastline, but if you are the kind of person who prefers being active over topping up your tan on the beach, there's also plenty of coastal walks that will keep you happy. For brisk walks with incredible vistas and fresh sea air, the 347 acres of Mendocino Headlands Park is an awesome place to go. The rocky bluffs overlook the Pacific Ocean, and you can find blackberry brambles and rose bushes around you as you stroll.

(www.parks.ca.gov/?page_id=442)

30. Ride the San Francisco Trolley to the Castro

It is no secret that the prices in San Francisco are rising, but there are still ways that you can enjoy yourself without breaking the bank. The public transport in the city can actually be a main attraction itself. The historic trolley cars can take you all the way to the trendy Castro district, which is the main LGBT area with plenty of fun bars where you can find a cheap cocktail to sip on. The trolley will wind you all the way through San Francisco, and it only costs $2 to ride.

31. Tuck Into Authentic Mexican Birria at El Parian

Since California is a state that borders Mexico, it should come as no surprise that you can find some of the most authentically delicious Mexican food in the country within California. Fish tacos abound, but if you want to try something a little different, we heartily recommend popping into El Parian in Los Angeles. This restaurant specialises in birria, which is the Mexican take on stewed goat meat. Whether you eat it as a stew, inside a taco, or inside a sandwich, it's never going to be bad.

(1528 W Pico Blvd, Los Angeles)

32. Swim in the Clear Waters of Aliso Beach

If you are travelling with kids and you would like to seek out the beaches of California that are most family friendly, we think that Aliso Beach in Orange County is always a great option. The waters here are clear and fairly calm, which means that your young children can have the experience of splashing in the ocean without danger. There are also some bonfire pits on the beach if you fancy having an alfresco dinner in the California fresh air.

33. Take a Selfie with the Giant Rock of Landers

Okay, so we know that you aren't going all the way to California just to see giant rocks, but the Giant Rock of landers really is something extra special because it's reportedly the largest freestanding boulder in the whole world. At a height of seven stories that covers an area of 5800 square feet, who are we to argue with the facts? Native Americans from the area also consider the huge rock to be sacred.

34. Take the Stairs Down Telegraph Hill

Telegraph Hill is one of the 44 hills of San Francisco, and a diverse neighbourhood that has seen immigrants, wealthy bankers, and artistic types living there. We recommend taking the bus to the top of the 284 foot hill, where you will find Coit Tower. But on the way back, it's a great idea to take the 400 steps. Alongside the path you'll find brightly coloured houses and gardens, and if you're lucky you might even spot a few of the wild parrots that live there.

35. Climb to the Top of Cathedral Peak

If you have already climbed the Half Dome inside Yosemite National Park, and you are looking for another hiking adventure, you should look no further than Cathedral Peak, a part of the Cathedral mountain range inside the park also. Actually, this is not so much a hike and more a climb, and you'll need some mountaineering experience under your belt if you would like to attempt this. Rappelling your way down is also an option for the adventurous at heart.

36. Look at the Elephant Seals of Piedras Blancas

Until recently, it was feared that the elephant seals could become extinct because they've been hunted for their oil rich blubber. But since the Marine Mammal Protection Act came into force, these beautiful and gentle creatures can now be seen living on the coast of California. The Piedras Blancas rookery is now home to 17,000 elephant seals, who come to the shore when it is time to mate. The best times to spot them are late October, late January, and late April.

(www.elephantseal.org)

37. Sip on Californian Beers at the Telegraph Brewing Company

California is wine country through and through. But if you would prefer so sip on a cool bottle of beer rather than a glass of wine, you don't have to miss out. At least not if you pay a visit to the Telegraph Brewing Company in Santa Barbara. This brewery creates American ales that are all made from locally sourced ingredients, so sipping on this beer is like sipping on the true taste of America.

(418 N Salsipuedes St, Santa Barbara; www.telegraphbrewing.com)

38. Visit the Monarch Sanctuary of Pacific Grove

If you are a lover of wildlife and the natural world, there's a good chance that you will have already heard of the Monarch butterfly, a North American butterfly that has to migrate south to survive the winter months. During those months, you can see the Monarchs in their thousands at Pacific Grove, which is now nicknamed Butterfly Town, USA. They cluster together on the pines and eucalyptus trees between the months of October and February.

(250 Ridge Rd, Pacific Grove)

39. Sip on Wines at Castello di Amorosa

For wine lovers, a trip to Castello di Amorosa might just be the highlight of a stay in California. This is a castle meets winery that is located close to Calistoga. Although the castle was actually completed this century, it's built in a traditional 13th century Tuscan style that makes it the most perfect place for at atmospheric glass of California wine. If you're feeling especially luxurious, be sure to stick around for their gourmet lunch options.

(4045 St Helena Hwy, Calistoga; www.castellodiamorosa.com)

40. Learn Something New at the Exploratorium

Travelling with kids is rewarding but not always the easiest experience. If you find yourself in San Francisco and you are unsure how to the keep the kids happy, the Exploratorium could be just what you are looking for. Otherwise known as the Museum of Science, Art, and Human Perception, this museum has over 1000 interactive exhibits. Some of the more interesting exhibits enable you to hear with your jawbone instead of your ear, and watch a live cow's eye dissection.

(Pier 15, The Embarcadero & Green St., San Francisco; www.exploratorium.edu)

41. Escape the Crowds at San Francisco's China Beach

San Francisco is mostly associated with bars, partying, and its bohemian atmosphere, but not necessarily for its awesome beaches. But if you find yourself in San Francisco and in need of a beach day, there are some options open to you, and we happen to like China Beach very much. The beach has its name because it was used by Chinese fisherman who used the bay as a campsite, but these days it's altogether more deserted, and a great place for a quiet swim.

42. Catch a Drag Show at Hamburger Mary's

If you find yourself in Los Angeles on a Friday night and you want to let your hair down in a comfortable environment, we think that you should head straight to West Hollywood, which is a huge stronghold for the city's gay community. One of the most iconic gay bars on the West Hollywood map is Hamburger Mary's, which is known for its friendly vibe and its incredible drag shows on every night of the week. For high kicks and hair higher than heaven, this is the place to be.

(8288 Santa Monica Blvd, Los Angeles; www.hamburgermarys.com/weho)

43. Have an Artsy Day at the Getty Museum

With 1.3 million visitors annually, the Getty Museum is one of the most visited museums anywhere in the world, and it's with good reason. This museum has one of the

most staggering collections of art to be found anywhere, with pieces ranging from the Middle Ages right up to the present day. A couple of the most famous works that can be found in the museum are Irises by Vincent Van Gogh and Angel of the Citadel by Marino Marini.
(1200 Getty Center Dr, Los Angeles; www.getty.edu/museum)

44. Hike to the Top of Yosemite's Half Dome

If you fancy yourself as an adventurer, there are plenty of incredible hikes across California, and hiking up the Half Dome in Yosemite National Park is one of the most incredible hiking challenges you can experience. The hiking time is 10-14 hours, and the elevation of the peak is 2695 metres, which means you need to set off early and be in great physical condition. Part of the mountain can only be ascended with cables, and this makes it a particularly intense adventure that's not for the faint hearted.
(www.nps.gov/yose/index.htm)

45. Swim in the Calm Waters of Bass Lake

If you are a water baby, there's certainly no shortage of coastline in California. But if you don't want to battle against the waves and would like an altogether calmer swimming experience, visiting Bass Lake, which lies just half an hour south of Yosemite National Park, would be a very good idea indeed. Because of the high elevation of this lake, the waters are blissfully warm in the summertime, with an average temperature of around 24 degrees Celsius.

46. Try Deep Sea Fishing Off the Coast of San Diego

If you love fishing, and you'd like to incorporate fishing of some kind into your holiday to California, San Diego is the place to be. And if you are accustomed to the tranquil waters of lakes and rivers, why not ramp things up a notch and try out deep sea fishing off the coast? These waters are particularly rich with Bluefin tuna and yellowtail, so why not have an adventure and see what you could catch?

47. Kayak Around Emerald Bay Beach

For peace and tranquillity, there is nowhere quite as relaxing as Lake Tahoe, the largest alpine lake in all of North America. Emerald Bay sits in a nook of the lake that guards its only island, Fanette Island. This secluded area is great for simply relaxing, but it's also very popular with people who like to kayak on the calm waters. You can paddle through the bottleneck of the bay, to the island, and along the sandy beaches.

48. Enjoy Classic Chicken and Waffles at Roscoe's

For a taste of classic Americana, you cannot beat a plate of chicken and waffles, and there is one place that is especially famous for this dish: Roscoe's. You can find Roscoe's restaurants all over the greater Los Angeles area, and Roscoe's is built solely on the idea of serving up good old fashioned chicken and waffles. The waffles are light and fluffy, the chicken is moist on the inside with crispy batter, and the coffee is strong enough to set your day off on the right foot.

(1514 North Gower Street, Los Angeles; www.roscoeschickenandwaffles.com)

49. Enjoy the Colours of the Antelope Valley Poppy Reserve

The poppy is the official plant of California, but you need to go to specific places if you'd like to see them at their very best. The Antelope Valley Poppy Reserve, as you might have guessed by the name of this state park, is one of the best places to check them out. The poppy fields here extend for an impressive 1750 acres, and are filled with brightly coloured orange poppies. On a visit to this park, you might just feel like you've been transported inside the set of the Wizard of Oz.

(15101 Lancaster Rd, Lancaster; www.parks.ca.gov/?page_id=627)

50. Watch an Outdoor Concert at LA's Greek Theatre

As the epicentre of the celebrity world, Los Angeles is the kind of place where you expect to be entertained, and we think that one of the very best spots for some entertainment underneath the stars is at the Greek Theatre, an open air amphitheatre that opened way back in 1929 and can seat over 5000 people. Thanks to the sunny California weather, it's possible to enjoy outdoor concerts here no matter the time of year.

(2700 N Vermont Ave, Los Angeles; www.lagreektheatre.com)

51. Get Cultural in Balboa Park, San Diego

When going to California, the cities of Los Angeles and San Francisco seem to get all of the attention, but we think that San Diego is very underrated, and you should try to get there if you can. Balboa Park is more than just another green space in the city. It's actually a cultural centre where you can entertain yourself for the day. In the park, you'll find no less than 15 museums, the San Diego Zoo, and some outdoor theatres and concert venues as well. *(www.balboapark.org)*

52. Explore Balconies Caves at Pinnacles National Park

With so many different landscapes, California is the place in the States to get back to nature, and something that you might want to explore are the many caves in California. While some of these are hard to explore without lots of spelunking experience, the Balconies Caves in Pinnacles National Park are the exception to the rule. The well marked Balconies Trail takes you directly to the caves so that you can explore easily.

(www.nps.gov/pinn/index.htm)

53. Indulge a Sweet Tooth at California Donuts

Sometimes, you need a sugar fix, and there's nothing that will quite hit the spot like a sugary pillow that is a doughnut. When that sugar craving hits, there is one place that we recommend going, and that's California Donuts in Los Angeles. They are open 24 hours a day, so you can get your doughnut fix whenever the craving strikes, and there are tonnes of flavours. We love the maple bacon and lucky charm encrusted doughnuts.

(3540 W 3rd St, Los Angeles; www.cadonuts.com)

54. Enjoy a Day Hike in Runyon Canyon Park

If you find yourself in glamorous Hollywood but you would like to escape some of the artifice and get back to nature, a wonderful place to do so is the Runyon Canyon Park, which lies just two blocks away from the famous Hollywood Boulevard. This 160 acre park is the perfect place to strap on your hiking shoes and get walking. There are 3 marked trails within the park, and the walk to Indian

Rock will give you an incredible 360 degree panoramic view.

(2000 N Fuller Ave, Los Angeles; www.lamountains.com/parks.asp?parkid=122)

55. Ride the Iconic Space Mountain Rollercoaster

One of the reasons that many families visit California is, of course, to visit the magical place that is Disneyland. And once you are inside this place of magic and fun, there is one rollercoaster that you simply have to ride: Space Mountain. This iconic rollercoaster is located within a giant dome that has a spaceflight theme. On the rollercoaster, you'll reach speeds of up to 45 kilometres per hour.

(1313 Disneyland Dr, Anaheim; https://disneyland.disney.go.com)

56. Get Close to Sea Life at the Santa Monica Pier Aquarium

If you would like to get close to California's incredible marine life without actually getting your feet wet, the Santa Monica Pier Aquarium is the place to be. Everything that you will see in this aquarium will come from the local waters, so it's a great opportunity to see what Californian waters really contain. Inside, you can find beautiful creatures, such as Leopard Sharks, Round Stingrays, and Purple Sea Urchins.

(1600 Ocean Front Walk, Santa Monica; https://healthebay.org/aquarium)

57. Watch a Baseball Game at the Dodger Stadium

If you are a sporty kind of person, it's well worth taking a day out to watch a sport's game while you're in California, which happens to host one of the most iconic stadiums in the world: the Dodger Stadium. This is the home ground of the LA Dodgers Baseball team, and whether you know a lot about baseball or not, getting a ticket for one of the games is a great idea to experience the atmosphere alone. The stadium can contain 56,000 spectators, so when it's full the atmosphere is electric.

(1000 Vin Scully Ave, Los Angeles; http://losangeles.dodgers.mlb.com/la/ballpark)

58. Hike Through the Unique Landscape of the Badwater Salt Flats

For a landscape like no other and that is guaranteed to take your breath away, you need to make your way to the saltwater flats of the Badwater Basin. Covering an expanse of 200 square miles, these are some of the largest protected salt flats that can be found anywhere in the world. It is possible to hike here and see the salt flats for yourself, but you should keep in mind that this is the lowest point of elevation in the western hemisphere, and that it's extremely hot and dry so it's best to try this hike in the spring and winter.

(www.nps.gov/deva/learn/nature/salt-flats.htm)

59. Dance the Night Away at Monarch, San Francisco

While you're in San Francisco, it's almost an obligation to party the night away, but with so many places to choose from, where should you take your dancing feet on a Friday night? We like a place called Monarch because on one floor you have a cocktail bar and in the basement a dance club, so you can have a little of whatever you like. And as the saying goes, a little of anything never hurt anyone.

(101 6th St, San Francisco; www.monarchsf.com)

60. Nibble on Decadent Macarons From Bottega Louie

When you're on vacation, it's the time when you can stop counting the calories and allow yourself to be more decadent than you would normally be. And we can't think of a better place to indulge than at Bottega Louie in West Hollywood. This gourmet patisserie has all kinds of dainty items that taste as good as they look, but it's the French macarons that always steal the show. The assorted macaron box with flavours like salted caramel and earl grey tea makes for a great gift.
(700 S Grand Ave, Los Angeles; www.bottegalouie.com)

61. Play Some Golf at Cypress Point Club

For many people, their idea of a perfect getaway doesn't involve lying on the beach or seeing dramatic landscapes, but simply hitting a few golf clubs in the sunshine. Luckily for you, the local people of California are rather fond of hitting the golf course too, and you won't have trouble finding world class golf clubs around the state. One we particularly like for its view of the ocean is the Cypress Point Club in Monterey.

(3150 17 Mile Dr, Pebble Beach; www.montereypeninsulagolf.com/Cypress-Point-Club)

62. Get Artsy at the Los Angeles County Museum of Art

While Los Angeles is more likely to be thought of as an entertainment city than an artsy city, culture vultures will have no problem finding some fine art to keep them happy on a trip to LA. One of the best places on the LA arts map is the Los Angeles County Museum of Art. The breadth of work on display is staggering, with works from ancient times to the present day. Key pieces include an 8th century Buddha figurine from India, and a selection of works by Picasso.

(5905 Wilshire Blvd, Los Angeles; www.lacma.org)

63. Take a Ride on the Palm Springs Aerial Tramway

For a view that you will not forget in a hurry, riding the Palm Springs Aerial Tramway, the largest rotating aerial tramway in the whole world, is a very good idea. This tramway will take you on a ride for two and a half miles along the stunning Chino Canyon and to the incredible wilderness of Mt San Jacinto State Park, which is so elevated that it's 30 degrees cooler than the desert floor. The tram cars rotate slowly as you travel so you can take in a complete panorama of this beautiful area. In the winter it's high enough to enjoy skiing when you get to the top.

(www.pstramway.com)

64. Explore the Desert Environment of the Living Desert Zoo & Gardens

Somewhere to explore the gorgeous desert environments of California is the Living Desert Zoo & Gardens, which can be found in the Palm Desert area in the Sonoran desert. This native wildlife zoo contains more than 450 local animal species as well as hundreds of local plant species in the desert botanical garden. There are hiking trails around the park if you are feeling active, or tram rides if you want to have a more leisurely visit.

(47900 Portola Ave, Palm Desert; www.livingdesert.org)

65. Celebrate the Southern Coast at the Urban Ocean Festival

The Aquarium of the Pacific on Long Beach hosts a very special and popular event each year: the Urban Ocean Festival. This festival is hosted at the end of April, and includes all kinds of awesome cultural activities right by the ocean. Some of the exciting things that you will encounter are an urban poetry reading competition, art viewings from local artists, outdoors theatre performances, pop-up shopping experiences, and great street food.

66. Relax in a Russian Bathhouse at Archimedes Banya

It probably isn't etched into your trip to San Francisco to visit a Russian bathhouse, but when you have weary feet and muscles and you need to escape the city streets for an afternoon, what could better than indulging in a spa experience? Archimedes Banya is a particularly special place because it takes on the ancient traditions of Russian bathhouses and Turkish hammams, so you get more than just a regular dip in a hot tub. The Russian saunas are very good for releasing toxins from the body.

(748 Innes Ave, San Francisco; www.banyasf.com)

67. Get a Great View of San Francisco from Coit Tower

San Francisco is a beautiful city, but from the street level it can be hard to appreciate just how picturesque it is. For us, the best place for a San Francisco view is from inside the famous Coit Tower, located in the cool Telegraph Hill neighbourhood of the city. The actual tower is very beautiful, designed with an art deco style, and it has beautiful frescoes all around the outside. From the observation deck, you can take in the whole city, and it's especially beautiful at sunset.

(1 Telegraph Hill Blvd, San Francisco; www.coittowertours.com)

68. Fill Your Stomach With Japanese Food in LA's Little Tokyo

One of the great benefits of visiting a cosmopolitan city like Los Angeles is that you have access to virtually every type of food you could ever hope to eat. For us, one of the highlights of any trip to the west coast is wandering around the city's Little Tokyo area, and putting as much

Japanese food into our mouths as possible. The sashimi lunch special at Sushi Gen is a delicious bargain, and the sea urchin creamy udon from Marugame Monzo is something extra special.

69. Go Strawberry Crazy at the California Strawberry Festival

The humble strawberry is one of those universally loved fruits that inspires joy and happiness, and what better way to get a strawberry fix than to attend a whole festival that is dedicated to the fruit? Well, there's good news, because the California Strawberry Festival, which is hosted in Oxnard every May, has now been running for over 30 years. Of course, you'll have the chance to sample all kinds of strawberry products, from strawberry funnel cake through to strawberry beers. Plus, there's eating contests, cooking demos, concerts, and arts and crafts.
(3250 S Rose Ave, Oxnard; http://castrawberryfestival.org)

70. Visit Famous Graves at the Hollywood Forever Cemetery

If you want to see the stars of Hollywood, you'll most likely walk on the Hollywood Walk of Fame, which is great, but something that you might not know about is the Hollywood Forever Cemetery, which as you might have guessed, is a place where you can find the tombstones of many a deceased celebrity. Some of the famous figures you'll find inside the cemetery include George Harrison and Gypsy Boots.

(6000 Santa Monica Blvd, Los Angeles; www.hollywoodforever.com)

71. Dive in the Clear Waters of Bluefish Cove

With so much coastline, you might expect the state of California to be a more famous diving location than it actually is. But if you are determined to see what's underneath the water on your trip to the state, fear not because there are some great diving spots, and Bluefish Cove might be the best of them all. This place is a sort-of secret, because it can only be accessed by boat, and that makes it all the more special. And it's especially rich in marine life too, so you are bound to see a lot underneath the water.

72. Sip on Cocktails at Louie's Gen Gen Room

San Francisco is a buzzing hub of bars and cocktail joints, so you'll have absolutely no problem finding a place to knock back a few swift drinks. But if it's cocktails that really get you going, we think that the best place in the city is Louie's Gen Gen Room. This is a small and cosy spot, and that's the whole charm of it. It really does feel like you're sipping on cocktails at a friend's place. The cocktail menu is also very creative. We particularly like Endless Summer – a mix of gin, Campari, sweet vermouth, and pineapple.

(871 Sutter St, San Francisco; www.liholihoyachtclub.com/gengen)

73. Enjoy all the Fun of the Los Angeles County Fair

The Los Angeles County Fair is one of the events on the LA calendar that people look forward to all year round. When the fair comes in around in September each year, thousands of locals and tourists descend upon the Fairplex in Pomona to enjoy all the fun of the fair. And this is not a fair as you have experienced one before. You will find thrilling outdoor rollercoasters and fairground rides, live

performances from world class bands, and some of the best food you'll find anywhere in California.
(http://lacountyfair.com)

74. Have a Hang Gliding Adventure at Dockweiler State Beach

There are tonnes of awesome beaches in California, and each of them has something special about it. If you prefer outdoor adventures to lazy beach days, the Dockweiler State Beach is a place that might interest you, because this is one of the best spots for hang gliding on the west coast. There is actually a hang gliding training park here, so you can have a go on the smaller 25 foot high dunes even if you are a total beginner.

75. Play Volleyball on Santa Monica Beach

The California coastline is home to some of the most beloved beaches in the world, and Santa Monica is one of these that you have no doubt already heard about. At a length of 3.5 miles, you won't have trouble here jostling for towel space. And if you fancy getting more active, this is one of the most popular beaches for a spot of volleyball.

There are nets dotted along the beach, so why not make some new friends by joining in with a game?

76. Visit the Majestic Vikingsholm Castle

As you stroll along the edge of Lake Tahoe and find yourself confronted with the dreamy Scandinavian design of Vikingsholm Castle, you could be mistaken for thinking that you have landed in the pages of a fairytale. The 38 room mansion was built in the 1920s by an aristocratic woman, and is loyal to many features of Scandinavian design, including six fireplaces inside. If you have any interest in architecture, the tour of the mansion will not disappoint.

(CA-89, Tahoma; http://vikingsholm.com)

77. Tuck Into Clam Chowder From Fisherman's Wharf, Monterey

California is a large state, and this means that each part of the state has slightly varying cuisines with its own specialities. If you make it over to Monterey, something that you won't want to miss is the delectable clam chowder. Fisherman's Wharf is one of the best places to chow down on all of this deliciousness, because as well as a piping hot bowl of chowder, you get an incredible view of the bay to go with it.

(1 Old Fishermans Wharf, Monterey; www.montereywharf.com)

78. Hike to the Hollywood Sign

The Hollywood Sign has to be one of the most iconic fixtures on the skyline of California, but instead of just looking at the sign from a distance, it's actually possible to hike up into the Hollywood hills and get above and beyond the sign. The Hollywood Sign is located within Griffith Park, and once you are there, there are three trails that you can take: Mt Hollywood Trail, Canyon Drive Trail, and Cahuenga Peak Trail. From the top, you can see out to the Pacific on a clear day.

79. Spend a Day Birdwatching in Point Lobos

There is tonnes of wildlife to be seen across California, and you absolutely shouldn't discount the number of birds you can see if you look to the skies. Whether you're a keen birdwatcher or you just fancy getting back to nature, the Point Lobos State Park is the place to be. Because this

state park is where the land meets the sea, you'll have the unique opportunity to spot seabirds as well as land birds. Sea birds regularly seen include the brown pelican and the black oystercatcher.
(www.pointlobos.org)

80. Down a Cherry Coke at a 19th Century Soda Fountain

Having opened way back in 1899, Watson's a is a precious piece of Californian history that is still functioning today. Back then, Watson's opened as both a drugstore and a soda fountain, but these days people just come for the sodas, the ice cream sundaes, and the classic American comfort food. A cherry coke or a root beer float is the way to go if you want to feel transported back in time.
(116 E Chapman Ave, Orange; www.watsonscafe.com)

81. Be Stunned by the Stark Landscape of Joshua Tree National Park

Located in the south of the state, the Joshua Tree National Park has some of the most unique landscapes that we have ever seen. This park combines the landscapes of two different deserts: the Mojave desert and the Colorado desert. In the most popular western part of the park, you'll find a stark landscape with hills of bare rock that are interspersed with loose boulders. Of course, you'll also find many Joshua trees dotted around too.

(www.nps.gov/jotr/index.htm)

82. Take in a Classic Movie at the Castro Theatre

Although there is a lot to see and do on the streets of San Francisco, sometimes all that you really want to do is watch a great movie in comfort, right? Well, luckily for you, one of the most impressive movie theatres in San Francisco is also a historic attraction. The building opened way back in 1922, and it has a stunning Spanish baroque façade. The inside is just as lavish, and with 1400 seats, you shouldn't have to worry about snagging yourself a ticket.

(429 Castro St, San Francisco; www.castrotheatre.com)

83. Learn Something New at the California Science Center

If you love to learn new things, there are plenty of museums and cultural centres in California, and we think that the California Science Center in Los Angeles is a really exciting place that will appeal to young and old alike. This is the west coast's largest hands-on science museum, and inside the museum you'll have the chance to get windblown in a hurricane simulator, see the insides of space capsules, operate a crash test dummy, and more.
(700 Exposition Park Dr, Los Angeles; https://californiasciencecenter.org)

84. Enjoy American Comfort Food From the Lobos Truck

Foodies on a trip to California will be able to fill their stomach night and day with all kinds of deliciousness, but if you can't afford to eat out at fancy restaurants for breakfast, lunch, and dinner, fear not because there are plenty of food trucks dotted around the state that dole out delicious grub on a budget. The Lobos Truck is one of our absolute favourites in Los Angeles, and it serves up great American comfort food like towering burgers and gooey mac n cheese.

(4470 Sunset Blvd #480, Los Angeles; www.thelobostruck.com)

85. See a Breath Taking Variety of Art at De Young

If your idea of a perfect getaway is hopping from gallery to gallery and taking in some breath taking works of art, you will no doubt be enamoured by the De Young, which is the fine arts museum of San Francisco. The museum opened way back in 1895, and since then has accumulated a huge collection of American art from the 17th century to the present day, including paintings, drawings, sculptures, and textiles. We love the room dedicated to 20th century couture, with pieces from the likes of Balenciaga and Yves Saint Lauren.

(50 Hagiwara Tea Garden Dr, San Francisco; https://deyoung.famsf.org)

86. Go Back in Time at the Old Sacramento State Historic Park

As you walk the streets of Los Angeles and San Francisco, you will probably have the impression that California is a dynamic and progressive place. While this is true, it's only one side of the story, and you can get to know traditional and historic California at the Old Sacramento State Historic Park. This is a place where you can find living history, and discover years gone by in a hands on way. Perhaps you'd like to take a ride on the old steam train, or shop for souvenirs in an old antiques shop?

(1014 2nd St #200, Sacramento; www.parks.ca.gov/?page_id=497)

87. Shop for a Vintage Outfit at Tavin

If you fancy yourself as something of a fashionista, the streets of Los Angeles have plenty to offer, but unless you want to look like every other person on your flight home you'll need to avoid the high street stores and shop in the vintage of boutiques of LA instead. One of the most enduringly popular of these boutiques is a shop called Tavin. Everything in here is very carefully selected, and has a floaty and bohemian feel, which is perfect if you're going onwards to Coachella.

(1543 Echo Park Ave, Los Angeles, CA 90026; www.tavinboutique.com)

88. Enjoy a Spot of Bass Fishing at Clear Lake

If your idea of the perfect holiday involves plenty of time sat at the edge of a lake with your fishing rod in the water, a trip to California will certainly not disappoint. For budding fishermen, we think that Clear Lake, which lies north of Napa County, is the best spot. This is the largest freshwater lake in all of California, reaching out for 68 miles of surface area. It's been nicknamed as the Bass Capital of the West, so your chances of scoring a huge catch is very good.

89. Discover an Incredible Art Collection at Norton Simon Museum

Located in Pasadena, the Norton Simon Museum is a little off the beaten track, but that makes it all the more charming, and it's a must visit for all art lovers who are in California. What's really incredible about this particular museum is the variety of items on display. You will find European tapestries in one room, Asian sculptures in another, and woodblock prints in another. We think that the religious paintings from India are something extra special.

(411 W Colorado Blvd, Pasadena; www.nortonsimon.org)

90. Learn the Art of Wine Blending at Wente Vineyards

It goes without saying that California is a wine lover's paradise, and at Wente Vineyards you can do more than just sip on great wines, you can actually learn the great art of wine blending. This winery is located in the lesser known Livermore Valley. In a session that lasts for around two hours, you will taste and evaluate the state blocks of wine to create your very own signature bottle of wine that you can take home with you.

(5565 Tesla Rd, Livermore; https://wentevineyards.com)

91. Get Grim at the Museum of Death

The idea of visiting a museum totally dedicated to death might seem like a grim thing to do on your holidays, but when you consider that the mission of the museum is to make people happy to be alive, you might start to think of it differently. Located in Hollywood, the Museum of Death contains the world's largest collection of serial killer artwork, photos of the Manson crime scenes, photos from the Dahlia murders, and lots more that's macabre and ghoulish.

(6031 Hollywood Blvd, Hollywood; www.museumofdeath.net)

92. Stroll the Venice Canals

When you make your way to the Venice area of Los Angeles, you could be forgiven for thinking that you have accidently found yourself in Europe instead of California. This area contains five picturesque canals that are about a quarter of a mile long each. Each one of the canals has sidewalks and bridges so that you can easily walk along them and escape the hustle and bustle of an otherwise very busy city.

93. Start Your Day With Coffee From Copa Vida

If you are the kind of person who cannot function without their first caffeine hit of the day, fear not because Americans are a nation of coffee drinkers and coffee lovers, and you'll be able to find a decent coffee wherever you go. A café that we like very much is Copa Vida in Pasadena. The owner has travelled the world to find the very best beans, and the staff are friendly even at the earliest hours of the morning.

(70 S Raymond Ave, Pasadena; www.cope-vida.com)

94. Have a Rock Climbing Adventure Up El Capitan

Yosemite National Park is more than just a place to experience some leisurely hikes. It's also a place where you can have heart-racing adventures, and rock climbing about the face of El Capitan would be something to really test your adventurous spirit. The rockface is totally vertical and reaches a height of 3600 feet, making it an iconic destination for keen mountaineers. Of course, this wouldn't be suitable for total beginners, but if you have some rock climbing experience you'll love it.
(www.nps.gov/yose/index.htm)

95. Peruse the Collections of the Huntington Library

Okay, so we know that you haven't trekked all the way to California to visit musty libraries, but you need to trust us when we tell you that the Huntington Library is something extra special. Located in San Marino, the collections here are something truly extraordinary. There is a European collection of 18th and 19th century paintings, an American

art collection, botanical gardens, a Chinese Garden, a Japanese garden with thousands of bonsai trees, and more.
(1151 Oxford Rd, San Marino; www.huntington.org)

96. Feast on Cherries at the Beaumont Cherry Festival

The humble cherry is a beautiful thing, and you can celebrate all of the glory of this fruit at the annual Beaumont Cherry Festival, which is hosted in the beginning of June each year. Of course, there will be cherries available to eat in many forms, from chocolate dipped cherries through to cherry liqueurs that help with the merriment. Plus there are parades, concerts, cooking demos, and lots more.

(http://beaumontcherryfestival.org)

97. Dance Through the Night at The Mayan

For partying right throughout the night, Los Angeles is, without a doubt, the city for you. There are endless clubs that you can choose to visit, but it's The Mayan in LA's downtown area where we keep going back for more. This was originally a theatre, which was remodelled to look like a Mayan temple, and now it's a place where people dance on every night of the week. With different music in every room, it's bound to be a place that pleases every music lover.

(1038 Hill St, Los Angeles; www.clubmayan.com)

98. Amuse Yourself on the Santa Cruz Beach Boardwalk

The Santa Cruz beach boardwalk is a place to relax, get away from it all, and that even the kids will enjoy. The park was founded in 1907, and this makes it the state's oldest surviving amusement park, which contains the Giant Dipper, one of the most famous wooden rollercoasters in the world. You can also enjoy old fashioned carnival games and try to win prizes, and chow down on beach snacks like toffee apples and candyfloss.

(https://beachboardwalk.com)

99. See the Coronado Shores Shipwreck

As everybody knows, California is a state that has lots of beautiful coastline, but there is more to the Californian coast than just sea and sand. If you would like to see something that's a little bit different, you can actually see some shipwrecks up close when you are in California, and one of the most visible is the Coronado Shores Shipwreck close to San Diego. This ship was actually a floating casino that ripped free of its anchor and blew onto Coronado island where it sank in 1937. When the tide is low, a large portion of the ship can be seen.

100. Watch the Waves Crash at the International Surf Festival

California has earned is reputation as the surf capital of the universe, but if you really want to soak up the local surf culture and take your surf appreciation to the next level, you need to go to the International Surf Festival that's hosted each August across the South Bay's beach cities. Of course, there's plenty of opportunities to ride the waves, and to check out pros from around the world showing what they've got. There's also volleyball and lifeguard competitions.

(www.surffestival.org)

101. Take in a Show at San Francisco's Great American Music Hall

Entertainment options are not hard to come by in San Francisco, but we think that the city's Great American Music Hall stands out from the crowd as something that is extra special. Dating back to 1907, this music hall is well known for its decorative balconies, columns, and frescoes that make it an atmospheric place to take in a show on a Friday night. There are all kinds of shows here, including jazz concerts, rock concerts, and even burlesque shows, so be sure to keep up with their programme of events.

(859 O'Farrell St, San Francisco; www.slimspresents.com/great-american-music-hall)

Before You Go…

Thanks for reading **101 Amazing Things to Do in California.** We hope that it makes your trip a memorable one!

Have a great trip!

Team 101 Amazing Things

Made in the USA
Columbia, SC
16 April 2019